D1403690

THE ALAMO

Joanne Mattern

Rourke
Educational Media

rourkeeducationalmedia.com

Before Reading:

Building Academic Vocabulary and Background Knowledge

Before reading a book, it is important to tap into what your child or students already know about the topic. This will help them develop their vocabulary, increase their reading comprehension, and make connections across the curriculum.

1. *Look at the cover of the book. What will this book be about?*
2. *What do you already know about the topic?*
3. *Let's study the Table of Contents. What will you learn about in the book's chapters?*
4. *What would you like to learn about this topic? Do you think you might learn about it from this book? Why or why not?*
5. *Use a reading journal to write about your knowledge of this topic. Record what you already know about the topic and what you hope to learn about the topic.*
6. *Read the book.*
7. *In your reading journal, record what you learned about the topic and your response to the book.*
8. *After reading the book complete the activities below.*

Content Area Vocabulary
Read the list. What do these words mean?

ammunition
chapel
emigrated
friars
immigration
memorial
missionaries
renovated
republic
ruins
scouts
sentry
siege

After Reading:

Comprehension and Extension Activity

After reading the book, work on the following questions with your child or students in order to check their level of reading comprehension and content mastery.

1. *What does renovate mean? (Summarize)*
2. *Why is the Alamo considered a symbol of freedom today? (Infer)*
3. *Why did the people of Texas want to renovate the Alamo? (Summarize)*
4. *Why would General Houston allow Santa Anna to live after he was captured by Americans? (Asking questions)*
5. *If Santa Anna was successful in his conquests, what could have happened to Texas? (Asking questions)*

Extension Activity

You are at the Alamo. General Santa Anna has just arrived with his men and are ready to fight. Write a speech that you will give to your men to get them ready for battle. What is important? What do they need to hear? What strength can you give them through your words? How can you support them? After you write your speech, grab a classmate and deliver your speech to him or her. Were they inspired?

TABLE OF CONTENTS

A WARNING CRY

February 23, 1836, was a quiet morning in the city of San Antonio de Bexar. Most of the people living there had already left. They knew danger was on its way.

Suddenly, at ten o'clock in the morning, the church bell began to clang. Everyone ran into the streets to see what was happening. A soldier looking out of the bell tower called down the terrible news. "The enemy is in view!"

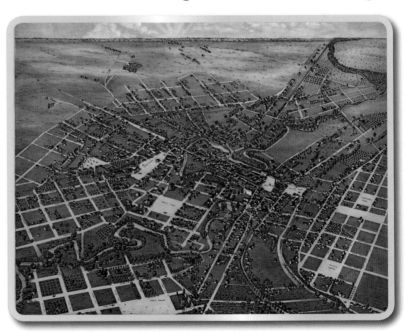

Map of San Antonio de Bexar.

Lieutenant Colonel William Travis was one of the two commanders of the Texian Army. He confirmed the news. No one was surprised. They had known for weeks that Mexican president General Antonio López de Santa Anna and his army were on their way.

The soldiers ran around town, grabbing everything they could. They grabbed clothes, rifles, **ammunition**, blankets, food, and tools. Then they hurried back to the town's fort, which was called the Alamo.

Antonio López de Santa Anna
1794–1876

Meanwhile, Colonel Jim Bowie, the other Texian Army commander, got a small group of soldiers and began looking for food. He found about 90 bushels of corn in nearby abandoned houses. Other soldiers rounded up a herd of cattle and brought them inside the Alamo's walls.

Colonel Jim Bowie
birth unknown–1836

Inside the Alamo, soldiers took position on the walls. After everyone was inside, the Alamo's gates slammed shut. About 157 men, along with 20 women and children, waited inside.

Freedom Fact!

The Texian soldiers called themselves "the Army of the People."

About 1,600 Mexican soldiers rode into town that day, with more to follow. The Alamo's defenders knew they were hopelessly outnumbered. Despite the odds, they held their positions. The battle for the Alamo was about to begin.

People reenact the Battle of the Alamo every year. These men are wearing Texian dress.

The uniformed Mexican soldiers were well-prepared and carried better weapons than the Texians.

THE ALAMO'S HISTORY

Before it became an American symbol, the Alamo was a home for Spanish **missionaries**. In 1718, an order of Catholic **friars**, called the Franciscans, came to the area to convert the Native American tribes to Christianity. The Franciscans built a structure where they could live and work. They called it the Mission of San Antonio de Valero.

The Alamo's Name?

No one is really sure how the Alamo got its name. Some people say the name comes from the many cottonwood trees in the area. "Alamo" is the Spanish word for cottonwood. Other people believe the name was used during the 1790s after a group of Spanish soldiers from Alamo de Parras in Mexico stayed there.

The Alamo

By 1793, most of the Native American tribes had converted to Christianity. A small town called San Antonio de Bexar had grown outside the mission. With their work done, the Franciscans abandoned the Alamo in 1793.

The Franciscans established missions throughout Texas.

In 1803, the Spanish began using the Alamo as a fort. The Alamo had thick, strong walls and a lot of space inside. There were many small rooms along the inside of the walls. However, the fort was so big, it took 1,000 men to defend it.

The Alamo had been built in the Spanish territory known as New Spain. In 1821, New Spain became an independent country called Mexico. Mexican citizens who lived in the north called the area Tejas, which would later be changed to Texas. By 1835, more than 20,000 people had settled in Texas. Many of these settlers had **emigrated** from the United States. They called themselves Texians.

Freedom Fact!

The strongest part of the Alamo was its **chapel**. The chapel walls were 4 feet (1.2 meters) thick and 22.5 feet (6.8 meters) tall.

This 1854 drawing shows what the Alamo chapel probably looked like in the 1830s.

Mexico didn't like the fact that so many people from another country were living on their land. In 1830, Mexico's government passed a law forbidding **immigration** from the United States. This upset the people living in Texas. In 1833, General Santa Anna became president of Mexico. Soon afterward, Santa Anna stopped following Mexico's constitution.

In 1822, Mexico's borders reached far north into modern-day Texas.

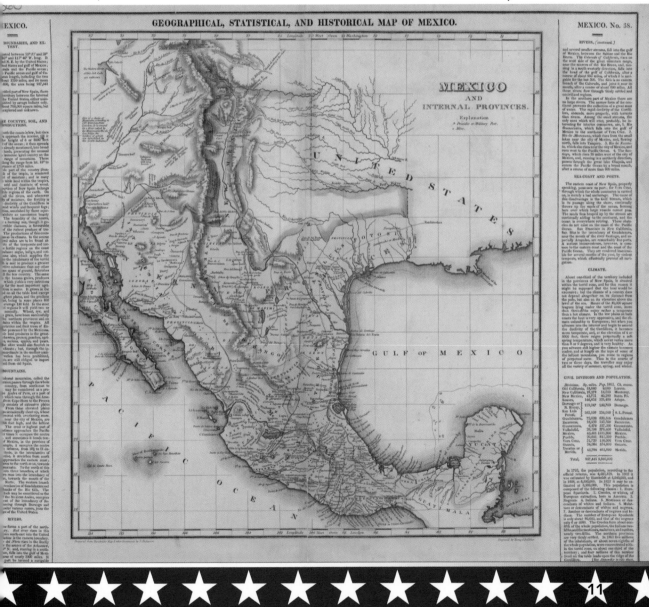

The Texians decided it was time to act. In 1835, they rebelled and formed a temporary government. Stephen Austin became the general of the new Texas army.

On October 12, 1835, Austin and a small army set out for San Antonio de Bexar to take the town from a Mexican army led by General Martin de Cos. General Cos had more than 800 men stationed in the Alamo and Texas. Instead of attacking, Austin's army laid a **siege** around the Alamo. When the Mexicans ran out of food, they would have to surrender. Meanwhile, Austin went to the United States to ask for help. A former officer in the U.S. Army named Sam Houston took his place leading the Texas army.

Stephen Austin
1793–1836

By December, Texas's Army of the People had grown to about 550 soldiers. On December 5, the Texians attacked the Alamo. By then, General Cos was out of food and didn't have enough ammunition to defend the fort. He surrendered on December 9.

The Army of the People celebrated defeating Mexico. They believed they had made Texas an independent nation. Most of the soldiers went home, thinking their job was done. They were wrong. As soon as General Santa Anna heard about what happened at the Alamo, he decided to personally stop the rebellion and take Texas back.

General Martin Perfecto de Cos
1800–1854

DEFENDING THE ALAMO

With the Army of the People gone, only 88 men were defending the Alamo by January 1835. Luckily, a few men dedicated to making Texas free were on their way. On January 19, Colonel Jim Bowie arrived at the fort with another thirty men. A few weeks later, Colonel William Travis arrived at the Alamo with another thirty men. Davy Crocket followed them shortly after.

William Travis
1809–1836

With Santa Anna's army approaching, most people left the town for safety. When a **sentry** spotted the army, two **scouts** rode out to spy on the Mexicans. They returned with alarming news. About 1,500 soldiers were headed their way! That afternoon, on February 23, the Mexican army entered San Antonio.

Since General Santa Anna couldn't surprise the Texians, he lay siege to the Alamo. Santa Anna had some of his soldiers hang a bright red flag in the bell tower of the church. This flag was a sign that Santa Anna wanted the Texians to surrender. If they did not, his army would attack.

Davy Crockett
1786–1836

Freedom Fact!

Santa Anna was merciless. He told his generals that he did not care how many Mexican soldiers were killed at the Alamo and that any Texian survivors would be killed.

Colonel Travis was not ready to give up. He fired a cannon to tell Santa Anna that the Texians would not surrender. However, Travis soon faced a big problem. His co-leader, Jim Bowie, was very sick and would not be well enough to fight. Travis was now in charge.

Days passed and the siege dragged on. Travis sent letters out of the Alamo, asking the leaders of Texas and the United States for help. Meanwhile, the Mexican army fired their cannons at the Alamo walls all day. Inside, the Texians waited for reinforcements. Only a small group of 32 men slipped into the Alamo on March 1. But no one else came. They would have to defend the Alamo on their own.

By early March, Santa Anna decided the siege had gone on long enough. It was time to attack.

Freedom Fact!

The guns used by the Texian army could only fire one bullet at a time. For this reason, soldiers kept several loaded guns nearby and had other weapons, like knives and swords.

"REMEMBER THE ALAMO!"

General Santa Anna's army attacked the Alamo at sunrise on March 6. The attack came so quickly that the sentries didn't have time to call a warning. Colonel Travis ran for the north wall with his shotgun in his hand. He fired at the approaching soldiers. A bullet immediately struck him in the head and killed him.

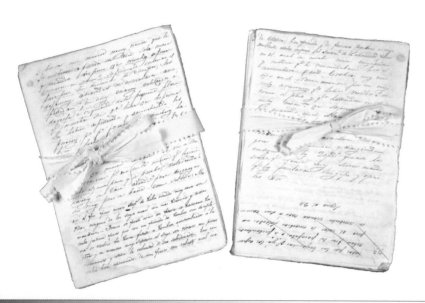

José Enrique de la Peña was a Mexican officer. He wrote about the Battle of the Alamo. These pages describe how William Travis died.

The soldiers loaded their cannons with nails, pieces of horseshoes, and broken tools. When the cannons fired, this scrap metal became deadly. The cannons were so lethal that the first waves of Mexican soldiers hid against the walls to avoid the onslaught.

When the Texians heard the shouts of the approaching Mexican army, they rushed to their positions to defend the fort.

Still, Santa Anna's troops kept coming. A wave of Mexicans attacked the north wall, where there were fewer Texian soldiers defending the fort. Mexican soldiers laid ladders against the walls and scrambled over the top. Other Mexicans ran to open the Alamo's gate. The Alamo was quickly overrun with Santa Anna's army.

The battle was over in an hour and a half. Following Santa Anna's orders, all of the remaining Texian soldiers were killed. A few Texian women and children survived, along with two slaves. The Mexicans let the women and slaves go free. Meanwhile, Santa Anna prepared his army to march to the east to attack other Texas forts.

Freedom Fact!

All of the Texian soldiers, fewer than 200 men, died at the Alamo. The Mexican army lost about 400 soldiers. Hundreds more were injured.

Santa Anna's Mexican forces greatly outnumbered the soldiers inside the Alamo.

The news of what happened at the Alamo traveled quickly. Texians were furious. They were now even more determined to defeat General Santa Anna and win their independence from Mexico. Hundreds of men hurried to join the Texian Army.

On April 21, 1836, General Sam Houston and about 900 soldiers were camped by the San Jacinto River. General Santa Anna marched his army of 1,200 men to within one mile (1.6 kilometers) of Houston's camp.

General Sam Houston
1793–1863

Freedom Fact!

*The Texas government declared that Texas was a free nation on March 2, 1836, during the siege of the Alamo. After the Battle of San Jacinto, Sam Houston was elected the first president of the **Republic** of Texas.*

Late that afternoon, General Houston and his army charged into Santa Anna's camp yelling their new battle cry, "Remember the Alamo!" The sleeping Mexican army was taken by surprise. More than 600 of Santa Anna's men were killed. Most of the rest were taken prisoner. The Battle of San Jacinto lasted about eighteen minutes.

Santa Anna escaped, but was captured the next day. Though many people wanted Santa Anna killed, Houston freed him after signing a document making Texas an independent nation.

In a surprise attack, General Houston's troops defeated Santa Anna's troops at the Battle of San Jacinto.

THE ALAMO TODAY

After the battle, the Alamo was in **ruins**. There were huge holes in the walls and signs of the battle were everywhere. A few months after the battle, most of the Alamo was torn down. Only the chapel, a building called the Long Barracks, and a few parts of the walls were left.

TEXAS: CHURCH OF ALAMO, SAN ANTONIO DE BEXAR.

The chapel is one of the few parts of the Alamo that was not torn down.

For many years, the U.S. Army used the Alamo only as a place to store supplies. Soldiers repaired the fort and added a second story. By 1878, the fort was too small for the Army's needs, so the Catholic Church took it over.

Freedom Fact!

In 1845, Texas became the twenty-eighth U.S. state.

By 1868, the Alamo was being used for storage by the U.S. Army.

Many people in Texas wanted the Alamo to be a place of honor. In 1883, the state of Texas bought the chapel from the Catholic Church. In 1905, an organization called the Daughters of the Republic of Texas bought the Alamo. They restored the grounds, the chapel, and the Long Barracks. In 1936, the entire site was **renovated** and reopened as a museum in honor of the one hundredth anniversary of the battle.

Freedom Fact!

The Daughters of the Republic of Texas is made up of the descendants of the people who fought for Texas's independence.

The Daughters of the Republic of Texas raised funds to restore the Alamo to its former glory.

Today the Alamo is known as "the Cradle of Texas Liberty." About 3 million people visit the Alamo every year. Visitors can learn about the battle and see artifacts and other treasures from the site. They can also see a **memorial** that includes statues and lists the names of the men who died defending the fort.

The Alamo remains a symbol of bravery and honor and an important place in American history.

TIMELINE

1718 —— *Mission San Antonio de Valero is established.*

1793 —— *The friars abandon the mission.*

1803 —— *Spanish soldiers occupy the Alamo.*

1830 —— *After the Mexican government forbids immigration from the United States, many people in Texas begin to talk about independence.*

1833 —— *General Antonio Lopez de Santa Anna becomes president of Mexico.*

1835 —— *Sam Houston becomes the leader of the Texian army on November 12.*

1835 —— *The Texian army defeats the Mexican army at San Antonio and takes control of the Alamo on December 9.*

1835 —— General Santa Anna assembles an army of more than 6,500 men to march on the Alamo on December 31.

1836 —— In late January and early February, Jim Bowie, William Travis, and Davy Crockett arrive at the Alamo with men to help defend the fort.

1836 —— Santa Anna and his army reach the Alamo on February 23, and begin a siege.

1836 —— Santa Anna's army captures the Alamo on March 6, killing all the soldiers inside.

1836 —— Sam Houston defeats Santa Anna's army at the Battle of San Jacinto on April 21.

1836 —— Sam Houston is elected president of the Republic of Texas on September 5.

1850 —— The U.S. Army rebuilds the Alamo.

1905 —— The Daughters of the Republic of Texas take over and restore the Alamo.

1936 —— The Alamo is renovated in time for the 100th anniversary of the battle.

GLOSSARY

ammunition (am-yoo-NISH-uhn): things that can be fired from weapons

chapel (CHAP-uhl): a small church

emigrated (EM-uh-grated): left your own country to live in another country

friars (FRY-urs): an order of religious men

immigration (im-uh-GRAY-shuhn): moving to another country to live there

memorial (muh-MOR-ee-uhl): something built or done to help people remember a person or event

missionaries (MISH-uh-nair-eez): people sent by a church or religious group to teach that group's faith to others

renovated (REN-uh-vay-ted): rebuilt and improved

republic (ree-PUB-lik): a form of government in which authority rests with voting citizens and is carried out by elected officials

ruins (ROO-inz): the remains of something that has been destroyed

scouts (SKOUTS): people sent out to bring back information

sentry (SEN-tree): a person who warns others of danger

siege (SEEJ): surrounding a place to cut off supplies until those inside have to surrender

INDEX

SHOW WHAT YOU KNOW

1. Why did Spanish missionaries build the Alamo?
2. From where had many settlers in Tejas, Mexico emigrated?
3. Why did Texian soldiers leave the Alamo after they defeated General Cos?
4. What did the Mexican army do to lay siege to the Alamo?
5. Why might people want to visit the Alamo today?

WEBSITES TO VISIT

www.thealamo.org
socialstudiesforkids.com/article/ushistory/alamobattle.htm
www.enchantedlearning.com/history/us/monuments/alamo

ABOUT THE AUTHOR

Joanne Mattern has written hundreds of books for children. Her favorite subjects are history, nature, sports, and biographies. She enjoys traveling around the United States and visiting new places. Joanne grew up on the banks of the Hudson River and still lives in the area with her husband, four children, and numerous pets.

Meet The Author!
www.meetREMauthors.com

www.rourkeeducationalmedia.com

PHOTO CREDITS: Cover © Natalia Bratslavsky, Library of congress, Percy Moran, Robert Jenkins Onderdonk; Title page © Shelley Davis; page 5 © LOC; page 6 © Texas State Library and Archives Collection; page 7 © neonriver; page 8 © Christopher Eng-Wong; page 10 © Wikipedia/Gleason; page 11 © H.C. Carey and I. Lea; page 14 © George Peter Alexander Healy/Wikipedia; page 15 © Chester Harding/Wikipedia; page 16 © newage, pzaxe; page 17 © arogant; page 18 © The University of Austin Texas; page 19 © LOC/Percy Moran; page 21 © North Wind Picture Archives; page 22 © Thomas Flintoff/The Museuem of Fine Arts, Houston/Wikipedia; page23 © JW1805/Wikipedia; page 25 © USTA Libraries Special Collection

Edited by: Jill Sherman

Cover design by: Nicola Stratford, nicolastratford.com
Interior design by: Renee Brady

Library of Congress PCN Data

The Alamo / Joanne Mattern
(Symbols of Freedom)
ISBN 978-1-62717-740-5 (hard cover)
ISBN 978-1-62717-862-4 (soft cover)
ISBN 978-1-62717-973-7 (e-Book)
Library of Congress Control Number: 2014935665

Printed in the United States of America, North Mankato, Minnesota

Also Available as: